Lizards

Other titles in the Nature's Predators series include:

NATURE'S PREDATORS

Lizards

Janet Halfmann

KIDHAVEN
PRESS™

THOMSON
———————— ✦ ————————™
GALE

San Diego • Detroit • New York • San Francisco • Cleveland
New Haven, Conn. • Waterville, Maine • London • Munich

© 2004 by KidHaven Press. KidHaven Press is an imprint of The Gale Group, Inc.,
a division of Thomson Learning, Inc.

KidHaven™ and Thomson Learning™ are trademarks used herein under license.

For more information, contact
KidHaven Press
27500 Drake Rd.
Farmington Hills, MI 48331-3535
Or you can visit our Internet site at http://www.gale.com

LIBRARY OF CONGRESS CATALOGING-IN-PUBLICATION DATA

Halfmann, Janet, 1944-
  Lizards / by Janet Halfmann.
    p. cm. — (Nature's Predators)
  Summary: Discusses the physical characteristics, habitats, behavior, how they hunt
and kill their prey, and predators of various lizards.
  Includes bibliographical references (p.   ).
  ISBN 0-7377-1887-0 (hardback : alk. paper)
  1. Lizards—Juvenile literature. [1. Lizards. 2.] I. Title. II. Series.

Printed in the United States of America

CONTENTS

CHAPTER ONE

Designed to Hunt

U nder the desert sun, a western whiptail lizard dashes across the sand from bush to bush. It searches for insects by sight and smell. Suddenly its jaws snap shut on an insect, which the lizard swallows in one gulp. Lizards like this western whiptail are among the world's most successful predators.

Lizards are **reptiles**, a class of animals with dry, horny **scales**. Other reptiles include snakes, turtles, and crocodiles. Lizards are the most abundant reptiles, with about forty-seven hundred **species** scattered around the world, especially in warm regions. Lizards live on every continent except Antarctica. They hunt from high in the trees in rain forests to underneath the sand in deserts. Some familiar types of lizards are geckos, iguanas, chameleons, skinks, and Gila monsters.

Lizard Bodies

Because lizards have many different homes and lifestyles, their bodies vary greatly in shape. The majority, such as the desert-hunting whiptail, are shaped like a slender cylinder. Tree-dwelling lizards, such as chameleons, are often flat from side to side like a leaf. Lizards that live in **crevices**, such as flat lizards, often have bodies squashed from top to bottom.

Lizards come in many sizes. The tiniest are the dwarf geckos of the Caribbean that can fit on a child's finger. At the other extreme, the bulky Komodo dragons of Indonesia grow to ten feet long. Most lizards measure between six and twenty-four inches in length.

Most lizards have four strong legs and clawed toes. Strong legs help lizards climb, leap, and make sudden dashes as they hunt. Many climbing lizards such as geckos and chameleons have specially adapted feet to give them a better grip as they hunt. **Burrowing** lizards do not need legs to hunt and often have tiny or no legs.

The majority of lizards have long tails. Long tails help lizards balance as they climb or run swiftly along the ground. The climbing chameleons can even hang onto branches with their tails, as monkeys do. On the ground, a long tail is especially important for balance in lizards that can run on two feet, such as collared lizards.

Strong Senses

Most lizards hunt primarily by sight. The majority of lizards have two keen eyes located at the sides of the

Like most lizards, the chameleon (pictured) hunts primarily by sight. Its keen eyes constantly look for prey.

head. (Another tiny third eye on top of the head is not for seeing. It helps the lizard regulate how much time it spends in the sun.) Lizards scan their surroundings, looking for movement. Once a prey moves, a lizard is very likely to spot it and grab it for dinner.

Excellent eyesight is especially important for lizards that hunt by lying in ambush and for lizards that hunt at night. The chameleon is an ambusher with exceptional eyes. Each eye can look in a different direction. While one eye scans for prey, the other checks for predators. Most geckos, unlike the majority of lizards, hunt at night. In order to see in the dark, geckos have huge

The Jacobson's organ, a pair of pits located on the roof of the lizard's mouth, helps lizards to smell prey.

eyes. In bright light, the gecko's **pupils** close into pin-holes or slits, similar to those in cats' eyes.

For many lizards a keen sense of smell is also vital for finding prey. Smell is especially important to lizards such as whiptails and skinks that actively search for prey. Lizards smell not only with their noses but with a pair of pits in the roof of the mouth called the **Jacobson's organ**. Several animals have this organ, including snakes, amphibians, and cats. The Jacobson's organ works together with the lizard's tongue to smell prey. Lizards flick out their tongues to pick up scent particles in the air or on the ground. The tongue then transfers the scents to the Jacobson's organ, which sends the information to the brain.

The Jacobson's organ is most developed in lizards with forked tongues, such as whiptails, beaded lizards, and monitor lizards. In these lizards the two tips of the tongue fit directly into the holes in the Jacobson's organ. The Jacobson's organ helps the lizard follow the prey's scent trail.

Powerful Jaws

Once lizards find prey, most species grab it with their powerful, quick jaws and sharp teeth. The jaws and teeth of most lizards are adapted for grabbing and holding on to prey rather than for chewing. For example the bite of the spiny lizard is so strong that it can support the lizard's own body weight for ten minutes. A few kinds of lizards, such as chameleons and horned lizards, grab prey with their tongues.

Sunbathers

Above all else, a lizard needs to be warm in order to hunt. A lizard that is cold can barely move. It is not able to catch prey, digest food, or escape predators.

Like all reptiles, a lizard's temperature is dependent on its surroundings. This is called ectothermic, which means "outside heat." It is also sometimes referred to as cold-blooded. People and other **mammals** and birds are **endothermic**, which means they heat themselves from within using energy from the food they eat.

When a typical lizard wakes up, it is cold and sluggish. To get warm, it stretches out in the sun or on a warm object to soak up heat. This is called **basking**. Each species has a preferred temperature at which it hunts, moves, and digests its food most efficiently. For most lizards, this temperature is between eighty-two and one hundred degrees Fahrenheit.

Many species can change their skin color to help them warm up or cool down. When a lizard is cold its skin becomes dark to let it absorb lots of heat. Then as the lizard warms up, its skin turns lighter to absorb less heat. The male common agama, or rainbow lizard, of Africa is a good example. On waking, its body is cold and a drab gray. Then as the lizard warms up in the sun, its head turns bright orange or red and its body purple or blue with yellow spots. Some lizards also change colors to show emotions such as anger or fear, similar to how a person blushes. The chameleons are the most famous color changers.

Lizard Anatomy

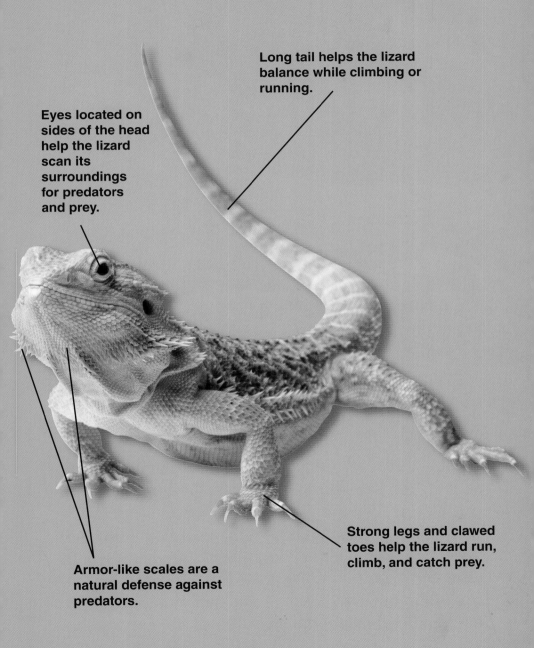

Long tail helps the lizard balance while climbing or running.

Eyes located on sides of the head help the lizard scan its surroundings for predators and prey.

Armor-like scales are a natural defense against predators.

Strong legs and clawed toes help the lizard run, climb, and catch prey.

The male agama lizard becomes bright red, orange, and blue as its body warms up in the sun.

A lizard's temperature determines when it is active. Early in the day, lizards usually bask in the sun. When they are warm they begin to hunt. Then when they get too hot, they find a shady spot to cool off. Later they bask again and resume hunting. In places with cold winters, lizards **hibernate** below-ground in burrows or crevices where it stays warmer. In extremely hot and dry areas, lizards also may rest belowground for long periods to keep cool and stay moist.

The Lizard's Diet

Since lizards do not use food to produce heat, they can survive on much less to eat than many other animals. The food that a bird eats in one day would last a lizard of the same weight a month or more.

Most lizards eat insects and small animals, such as birds, mice, and other lizards. But larger lizards prey on animals as big as water buffalo. Many lizards also eat eggs. While most lizards eat a variety of prey, some are fussy. The horned lizards in dry areas of western North America and Mexico eat mostly ants. An Australian snake lizard feasts mostly on scorpions.

No matter what kind of food a lizard seeks, it is a very successful hunter. Lizards have been hunting and gulping down meals since the time of the earliest dinosaurs 200 million years ago.

CHAPTER TWO

Hunting by Sight and Smell

Lizards hunt mostly by day but also by night. Some are sit-and-wait predators, patiently watching to ambush prey that come near. Others hunt on the move, actively searching for prey. But whatever a lizard's hunting style, insects and other prey should be wary. Lizards, with their keen senses of sight and smell, are some of the most successful hunters on Earth.

The Sit-and-Wait Ambushers

Several families of lizards are primarily sit-and-wait ambushers. They include chameleons, chisel-teeth lizards, and iguanas. These hunters perch motionless in the places prey congregate, such as in trees, bushes, and near anthills. Sit-and-wait ambushers locate prey mostly by sight. Once prey is spotted, ambushers either dart out and capture the prey with their jaws or snatch it with sticky tongues.

The chameleons are the champion sit-and-wait ambushers. Most of the world's chameleons live in trees and bushes in the forests of Africa and Madagascar. Chameleons move very slowly, have no ears, and can barely smell. They hunt by day, relying on their big eyes to spot an insect's slightest movement.

The hunting chameleon perches motionless on a branch. Its flat shape makes it look like a leaf fluttering in the breeze. The chameleon clamps on to its

Lizards are fierce predators, often preying on other lizards. Here, a collared lizard ambushes a gecko.

branch tightly with joined-together toes—some facing forward and others backward. The lizard's bulging eyes swivel, one eye looking forward for prey and the other backward for danger. When an insect is spotted, the chameleon creeps slowly toward it, then stops several inches away. Focusing both eyes on the insect, the chameleon judges the distance. Then, aiming with its entire head, the chameleon gets ready to strike.

In the blink of an eye, the chameleon's long, slender tongue shoots out of its mouth. Chameleons can extend their tongues as far as twelve inches, or two-and-a-half times the length of the head and body. Most of the time the hollow tongue lies bunched up around a special tongue bone in the lizard's mouth. When the chameleon is ready to strike, muscles shoot the tongue out of the lizard's mouth. The tip of the tongue is covered with sticky saliva. When the tongue hits the insect,

Chameleons snatch prey with their long, sticky tongues.

the end becomes a suction cup that grabs the prey. The largest chameleons can snatch birds with their strong tongues.

Not all ambushers are slow like the chameleon. The leopard lizard is a speedy desert dweller of the western United States and Mexico. The leopard lizard is about twelve inches long and is tan or white with brown spots. In the daytime the leopard lizard hides motionless in the shadows under bushes waiting for unsuspecting large insects and smaller lizards. It flattens itself against the ground, where its spotted body blends in with the soil. When a grasshopper lands on the bush to nibble, the leopard lizard crawls slowly toward it. Then suddenly the lizard uses its strong legs to pounce, grabbing the grasshopper with quick, powerful jaws.

The Active Wanderers

Several other lizard families hunt primarily on the move, actively probing and digging for prey. They include skinks, whiptails, and monitor lizards. These lizards search for prey not only with their eyes, but also rely heavily on their sense of smell. Whereas sit-and-wait ambushers usually flick their tongues little or not at all, wandering lizards flick their tongues frequently to smell the air and ground.

Skinks make up a large family of lizards that hunt on the move. They are sleek and have smooth, shiny scales. They hunt during the daytime in **habitats** ranging from deserts to forests.

This skink uses its colorful blue tongue to pick up the scent of prey.

The five-lined skink is common in moist wood-lands of the United States. It is about six inches long from head to tail. After basking on a sunny log or rock, the skink darts about searching for insects close to its burrow or other hiding place. As it hunts, the five-lined skink's tongue and nose are busy. The skink's slightly notched tongue flicks out, picking up smells. Its nose presses against the ground or trunks of trees. When the skink finds an insect, it grabs it with its jaws.

The large caiman lizards of South America also move about searching for prey, but they hunt underwater. Caiman lizards are members of the whiptail family. Caiman lizards, which can grow to four feet long and resemble crocodiles, are good swimmers and live in flooded forests and near slow-moving streams. They have long, deeply forked tongues for smelling prey. Their favorite food is snails.

The hunting caiman lizard walks on the bottom of streams. It uses its large head and blunt, rounded snout to turn over stones and leaves to search for snails. At the same time, the lizard flicks its long, sensitive tongue to pick up the snails' smell. To help with the search, the lizard scratches away at leaves and dirt with its feet. When the caiman lizard finds a snail, it grasps it with its powerful jaws. The caiman lizard has one of the most powerful pairs of jaws of all lizards. Its jaw muscles are especially large. The lizard picks up a snail like a nut in a giant nutcracker.

Saliva Full of Bacteria

Komodo dragons, the largest and most ferocious lizards, have a special weapon to bring down prey—saliva filled with deadly bacteria. Komodo dragons belong to the monitor lizard family, a group that includes many of the largest lizards. The clay-colored Komodo dragons live on a few Indonesian islands.

A Komodo dragon hunts prey as large as deer, wild boars, and water buffalo. The giant lizard grabs its prey with its huge jaws and bites it repeatedly, sending saliva with bacteria into the wound. Even if a bitten prey

With every bite from its razor-sharp teeth (shown), the Komodo dragon sends saliva filled with deadly bacteria into its prey.

escapes, it has no chance of surviving. In a few days, the bacteria makes the animal sick and weak. Then the Komodo dragon easily delivers the final killing bite.

Nighttime Hunters

Most lizards are daytime hunters, but in deserts and other warm regions large groups of lizards hunt at night. In these regions the warm air keeps the lizards at their preferred temperature. Night hunters include most geckos, snake lizards, night lizards, and some beaded lizards.

Geckos live in warm areas around the world and hunt just about anywhere, even in houses. The tokay gecko is commonly found in houses in Southeast Asia. This large gecko measures about twelve inches long and is blue gray sprinkled with orange spots. Tokay geckos live behind cupboards and picture frames or in the roofs of village houses. At night they come out to hunt moths and other large insects. The insects are no match for the geckos. Geckos have special toe pads that let them run up windows and upside down across ceilings, just like flies. The toe pads are covered with thousands of hooklike hairs that work much like Velcro.

The hunting tokay gecko hides in a shadowed area of the wall or ceiling. Its catlike pupils open wide in the darkness to give it excellent vision. When the gecko spies an insect, it darts from its hiding place and snaps up the prey with its powerful jaws.

Whether waiting in ambush or wandering about searching for prey, lizards usually get their target. And once in a lizard's grasp, a prey has little chance of escaping.

CHAPTER THREE

The Kill and the Feast

Lizards are not delicate when it comes to eating their prey. Once a lizard grabs its prey and crushes it with its strong jaws and teeth, it is dinnertime. Most lizards swallow their prey whole or in large chunks since their teeth are not adapted for chewing.

Handling Difficult Prey

Sometimes a prey needs special handling before a lizard can crush and swallow it. For example the jaws of the eastern fence lizard can only grab one end of a long, bulky insect **larva** such as a caterpillar. So the lizard shakes the larva violently to break it into pieces. Then the lizard picks up the parts one by one. A wasp nest found by a skink also gets a good shaking. The skink holds the nest in its jaws and shakes it until it breaks apart and the babies fall out. Then the skink gobbles up the babies to eat.

Other times, captured prey struggle and need to be subdued before they can be eaten. The side-blotched lizard of the United States and Mexico preys on large, active grasshoppers and moths. The lizard holds the moving insects in its jaws and beats them back and forth against the ground to kill them. The tokay gecko does much the same thing with bird and lizard prey that are too bulky to kill by biting. Deer and goats captured by the Komodo dragon almost always put up a fight. To kill them, the Komodo bites them repeatedly and shakes them from side to side, like a dog with a slipper.

A grasshopper struggles to free itself from a tokay gecko's crushing jaws.

The Gila monster (above) and the Mexican beaded lizard (inset) are the only poisonous lizards in the world.

Poisonous Bite

Only two species of lizards in the world have a poisonous bite. They are the beaded lizards: the Gila monster and the Mexican beaded lizard. The Gila monster lives in the southwestern United States and nearby Mexico. It grows to twenty inches long and is the largest lizard in the United States. The larger Mexican beaded lizard lives in western Mexico and Guatemala. Both species are primarily desert animals. The Gila monster is pink and black, and the Mexican beaded lizard is mostly black with cream markings.

Both species have a broad, flat head; a bulky, round body; short, powerful legs; and a stocky tail, where fat is stored for when food is scarce.

The poison or **venom** is produced in glands in the lower jaw. Unlike snakes, which produce venom in the upper jaw, beaded lizards cannot inject venom into their prey. Instead the venom flows into the grooves of the lizard's teeth. As the lizard bites its victim, the venom seeps into the deep wound.

Mealtime

Before swallowing their prey, some lizards retreat to a safe or shady spot. For example the tokay gecko usually goes back into the shadows to eat its prey. The Komodo dragon may drag its prey into the bushes.

A fearless monitor lizard attacks a snake. Lizards use their powerful jaws to crush their prey.

Lizards generally crush their prey before swallowing it. To crush it, they bite it with their sharp teeth and powerful jaws. They also smash the prey between the tongue and the top of the mouth. Lizards often bite and crush their prey repeatedly. The tongue is used to move the prey within the mouth and back into the throat for swallowing. Prey are usually swallowed headfirst.

Komodo dragons and other monitor lizards rip large prey like goats and deer into huge slices before swallowing them. These lizards have large, curved, sharklike teeth specialized for slicing off slabs of flesh. First the Komodo dragon rips open the animal and eats

Komodo dragons rip chunks of flesh from an animal and swallow them whole.

its insides. Then the dragon slices slabs from the prey by biting with its teeth while jerking backward with its entire body. The Komodo dragon gulps down the enormous chunks whole, bones and all.

The Komodo dragon can swallow huge chunks because its lower jaw is very flexible. The Komodo can unhinge its lower jaw from its skull, as snakes can, to swallow extremely large prey. The Komodo dragon can swallow the entire head of a wild boar in one gulp.

Big Mouth

While other lizards cannot match the gape of the Komodo, they can open their jaws very wide. This is due to several movable **joints** in the skull and jaws, especially one that lets the lower jaw move freely. In some lizards, the upper jaw also can bend. Lizards can generally swallow anything with a diameter less than the width of their heads. For lizards with large heads like the leopard lizard, that means a big mouthful. A scientist watched a female leopard lizard swallow whole a desert iguana more than three-quarters its own size. It took the leopard lizard three hours to get the iguana down its throat.

The leopard lizard is not alone in eating large meals. The Australian thorny devil has been known to eat up to twenty-five hundred ants at one sitting. The Gila monster can eat up to 35 percent of its weight at one meal. Komodo dragons are some of the biggest eaters of all. In one meal a Komodo dragon ate a wild pig just slightly smaller than itself.

Special Eating Techniques

Some lizards have special eating techniques. For example, eggs are a favorite food of many lizards. But lizards do not swallow eggs whole as they do most of their prey. The Nile monitor is a well-known egg predator. It uses its long, sharp claws to dig up the nests of crocodiles to get to their eggs. The Nile monitor takes one egg at a time from the nest. With its head slightly raised, the lizard turns the egg in its mouth to pierce the egg's shell. The lizard then lets the liquid run down its throat.

Most lizards do not chew their food, but chameleons are an exception. The chameleon's chewing is automatic. As soon as its tongue snaps back into its mouth, the chameleon starts chewing with its small teeth. In fact chameleons chew even if the prey they were after gets away and they can still see it. While the chameleon chews its prey, it is busy looking for the next insect to ambush.

The snail-loving caiman lizards have special teeth for smashing hard shells. These lizards have flat, molarlike teeth at the back of the mouth. After grabbing a snail with its jaws, the caiman lizard emerges from the water and lifts its head to let the snail fall to the back of its mouth. There the large flat teeth and powerful jaws crack the snail's shell into many pieces. The lizard removes the shell pieces from its mouth with its tongue. Then it swallows the soft part of the snail.

Cleaning Up

Both during and after meals lizards often groom themselves. Geckos use their tongues to carefully clean their

The flat-tailed gecko uses its tongue to clean sand from its eyes.

faces, including their eyeballs. The European glass lizard definitely needs an after dinner face wash. This lizard eats snails—shells and all. After gulping a snail, the lizard rubs its nose along the ground to get rid of the slime. The Komodo dragon takes time between large gulps to lick its chops with its thin, yellow tongue. Later the Komodo coughs up pellets containing the parts of the prey that it cannot digest, such as hair, teeth, hooves, and bones.

Grab, crush, gulp is the lizards' way of eating. It may not be fancy, but it has served lizards extremely well for a very long time.

CHAPTER FOUR

Avoiding Danger

L izards are highly skilled predators, but they also make tasty meals for many larger animals. Mammals that eat lizards include coyotes, badgers, and foxes. Lizards also are eaten by hawks, owls, roadrunners, and other birds. Lizards are the favorite food of many snakes, including the spotted leaf-nosed, which eats little else. In addition large lizards often eat smaller ones, especially the young.

Hiding from Predators

Like most animals, the main way lizards stay safe is by avoiding being seen. When resting, lizards hide in burrows and crevices and under stones and other objects. To stay safe while basking and hunting, most lizards are colored to match their surroundings. For example, many desert hunters are light colored to match the sand, while lizards that hunt in trees are often green.

Many lizards also have blotches, stripes, or bands to break up their outlines so they will merge into the background. This is similar to the **camouflage** uniforms worn by soldiers. The desert-dwelling horned lizards are a perfect example. Most are brown with dark blotches. To blend in even more the horned lizards flatten their pancake-shaped bodies against the sand.

Fleeing from Predators

If a lizard is detected by a snake or bird of prey, it will usually flee. Most lizards hunt close to their hideouts. If a lizard sees or smells a predator, it dashes for its burrow or another hiding place. As extra protection, the prickle-tail lizard of South America and several others

Lizards are a favorite food of many larger animals, including snakes.

The basilisk lizard has specially designed toes that enable it to run on top of water.

block the entrances to their hideouts with their spiny or fat tails.

Lizards that live in trees climb to higher branches to escape. Often they move around to the opposite side of a tree trunk to hide, much like squirrels do. The slow-moving chameleons simply drop to the ground or a lower branch, then resume their motionless position.

The flying dragons and flying geckos of Southeast Asia become gliders to escape predators. These lizards leap from their perches and glide through the rain forest, much like flying squirrels. The dragons glide on ribbed wings that open like umbrellas, and the geckos stretch out folds of skin along their sides like parachutes.

Most lizards that hunt on the move are fast runners. Some, such as the leopard lizard and the basilisk lizard, can run upright on two feet. The basilisk lizard has special toes that even let it run on top of water.

Some lizards escape by diving—in water or sand. Asian water dragons and sailfin lizards often bask on branches above rivers or lakes. When a predator threatens, they dive into the water. Fringe-toed lizards have comblike scales on their toes that let them run easily across sand without sinking. If a roadrunner or badger approaches, the lizards plunge into the sand and disappear.

Take My Tail

Sometimes a lizard is unable to flee because it is surprised by an enemy. Then the lizard must use other

Lizards are able to break off their tails when would-be predators threaten them.

methods to defend itself. Most lizards are too small to win a fight against a larger animal, so they have developed other tactics. The most well-known defense is breaking off the tail. Lizards can break off their tails by contracting their muscles. Special weak bones in the tail let it break off easily. Muscles in the broken-off tail keep it wriggling about to distract the predator. Meanwhile, the lizard sneaks away.

The long tail of a lizard called the glass snake confuses its hawk predators even more. The glass snake's tail breaks into many pieces, like shattered glass. While a hungry hawk chases piece after wriggling piece, the glass snake makes a fast getaway.

Lizards begin to grow a new tail almost immediately. New tails take a few months to grow and are usually shorter, thicker, and paler than the original.

The western banded gecko uses its striped tail to distract a predator's attention away from its head.

Shedding the tail is so common that in some species a lizard with its original tail is hard to find.

Since tail loss works so well as a defense, some lizards tease predators into attacking their tails. These lizards have brightly colored or boldly patterned tails. The flashy tails take attention away from the lizard's head and other important body parts. For example, the tail of the western banded gecko has dark brown and tan stripes. When a snake approaches, the gecko raises its tail and wiggles it about.

Young lizards, which are in the most danger of being eaten, often have the flashiest tails. The young of some woodland skinks of Australia have bright red tails that they twitch as they hunt. Most young North American skinks have bright blue tails that break off easily.

Goo, Blood, and Poop

Lizard tails and other body parts protect their owners in other ways. Several kinds of Australian geckos can shoot threads of sticky, smelly mucus from pits in their tails. The threads travel up to twelve inches and snare predators such as large spiders and snake lizards in a cobweblike trap. The predators cannot move and the gecko gets away. Some species of horned lizards can squirt a thin stream of red blood from their eyes. The blood can shoot four feet, over and over again. The blood tastes bad if it gets in a fox's or coyote's mouth and also irritates the predator's eyes. Alligator lizards have a gross surprise for snakes or birds that snatch them. The lizards try to smear the predators with poop.

The frilled lizard of Australia can puff out its frilled collar to bluff an animal much fiercer and larger than itself.

A Mouthful of Spines

Several lizards protect themselves with hard, sharp spines. Spines make an animal difficult to swallow, and many predators avoid spiny prey. The armadillo lizard of South Africa is a small, slow-moving lizard that is covered with spines from head to tail. Like its name-sake, the armadillo, it can roll itself into a ball. If surprised by a snake or bird of prey while hunting, the armadillo lizard grabs its tail in its mouth and rolls into a spiky ball. The sungazer from southern Africa is another spiny lizard. If threatened, it lies flat on the ground, presenting a predator with only spines. If the predator does not leave, the sungazer strikes with its spiny tail.

Call My Bluff

Several lizards are amazing bluffers. They make themselves look much bigger and fiercer than they really are, a tactic that often startles predators and scares them away. The most spectacular bluffer is the frilled lizard of Australia. It has large flaps of skin that usually lie folded around its neck like a cape. But when an eagle or larger lizard threatens it, the frilled lizard flares the flaps into a huge, brightly colored ruffle almost as wide as the lizard is long. At the same time, the lizard rears up, opens its mouth wide, and hisses.

The Komodo dragon and other large monitor lizards not only bluff like their smaller relatives, but they have powerful weapons besides. If the Komodo dragon's puffing up and hissing do not work, it bites with sharp teeth, scratches with long claws, and lashes its powerful whiplike tail.

The Komodo dragon, as the largest animal on the islands where it lives, rules supreme. It has little to fear from predators. Other lizards are not so lucky, but they have been extremely successful nonetheless for millions of years. Lizards big and small, with all their defenses and keen senses, are likely to remain the most numerous reptiles on the planet.

GLOSSARY

basking: Warming the body by lying in the sun.

burrowing: Tunneling under the ground.

camouflage: To blend in with the surroundings.

crevices: Narrow openings in the Earth or between rocks.

ectothermic: Having a body temperature that is dependent on the surroundings; also called cold-blooded.

endothermic: Having a body temperature that is controlled by internal body systems; also called warm-blooded.

habitats: The natural homes of plants or animals.

hibernate: To spend the winter sleeping.

Jacobson's organ: Small pits on the roof of a lizard's mouth used to smell and taste.

joints: The parts of the skeleton that act like hinges where bones meet.

larva: A baby insect, which often has a soft body and looks like a worm.

mammals: Animals that nurse their young with milk from mammary glands.

pupils: The openings in the middle of the eyes that let in light.

reptiles: Animals that are ectothermic, have a backbone and dry, horny scales, and are adapted to living on land. Reptiles include lizards, snakes, turtles, and crocodiles.

scales: Plates forming the outside covering of snakes and lizards.

species: A group of animals or plants that share similar characteristics and can mate with one another.

venom: The liquid poison produced by some animals.

FOR FURTHER EXPLORATION

Books

Margery Facklam, *Lizards Weird and Wonderful*. New York: Little, Brown, 2003. This colorfully illustrated book takes a close-up look at several kinds of lizards, such as the Komodo dragon and the chameleon. A chart compares the characteristics of lizards, snakes, and salamanders.

Joanne Mattern, *Lizards*. New York: Benchmark Books, 2002. Using photos and informative text, this book describes the characteristics and lives of lizards. The book also takes the reader through a lizard's day and discusses the relationship of lizards to people.

Trudi Strain Trueit, *Lizards*. New York: Childrens Press, 2003. Using easy-to-read text and colorful photos, this book discusses the characteristics of lizards and how they live and defend themselves.

Video

Growing Up Wild: Leaping Lizards, Alexandria, VA: Time-Life Video, 1992. Shows a close-up view of the characteristics and behavior of lizards and other reptiles living around the world.

Websites

Animals of the Rainforest (www.animalsoftherain forest.com). This website created by sixth-grade science classes has wonderful photos of a variety of lizards and lizard facts researched and written by students.

Desert USA: Desert Animals & Wildlife (www. desertusa.com/animal.html). Includes photos and descriptions of the Gila monster and some other lizards that live and hunt in the deserts of the United States.

Global Gecko Association: Gecko Sounds (www. gekkota.org/html/gecko_sounds.html). Contains the calls made by three very different sounding geckos, including the tokay.

Nature: The Reptiles: Lizards/PBS (www.pbs.org/ wnet/nature/reptiles/lizards.html). Includes several photos of lizards, a discussion of lizards as pets, and a list of lizard resources.

San Diego Natural History Museum: Reptiles (www. sdnhm.org/exhibits/reptiles/index.html). This website contains numerous photos and resources about lizards and other reptiles.

Sedgwick County Zoo: Animals (www.scz.org/ animals/home.html). This website features several lizards, including the Komodo dragon, the Gila monster, geckos, and a chameleon.

INDEX

PICTURE CREDITS

ABOUT THE AUTHOR

Janet Halfmann has written many nonfiction books for children and young adults, most of them on animals and nature. Her books include a six-title series on wildlife habitats and several books on the lives and behavior of insects and spiders. This is her second book in the Nature's Predators series. Her first book was on scorpions. She also wrote *The Tallest Building* for the Extreme Places series of KidHaven Press.

The wonders of nature have intrigued Halfmann from the time she was a child growing up on a farm in Michigan. She is a former daily newspaper reporter, children's magazine editor, and children's activity book writer and editor. When she is not writing, Halfmann works in her garden, explores nature, and spends time with her family.